GEORGE
WASHINGTON
COLORING BOOK

Peter F. Copeland

DOVER PUBLICATIONS, INC.
Mineola, New York

*To Rachel Watson
and Burwell Bassett*

Bibliographical Note

George Washington Coloring Book is a new work, first published by
Dover Publications, Inc., in 2003.

International Standard Book Number

ISBN-13: 978-0-486-42647-1
ISBN-10: 0-486-42647-5

Manufactured in the United States by Courier Corporation
42647506
www.doverpublications.com

Introduction

George Washington will forever be known as the beloved "Father of Our Country," thanks to his instrumental role in the shaping and birth of the United States. In an age crowded with larger-than-life figures—including Frederick the Great, Voltaire, Rousseau, and Catherine the Great—Washington stands apart as a unique and unforgettable hero to his people.

Born and raised among the wealthy slave-holding aristocracy of Virginia, Washington became a skilled military strategist and soldier, as well as a strong opponent of British restrictions on colonial lifestyle and trade. During this critical period in this nation's history, Washington stood for and defended the republican precepts of government. He was active in movements to gain independence from British rule, first as a Virginia delegate to the Continental Congress, and later as Commander-in-Chief of the Continental Army. After eight years in battle, Washington led his troops to victory and won the Revolutionary War.

Washington's actions on the field and in political chambers are an exhibition of iron determination and tireless valor. As the first president, and the only one to be unanimously elected by the Electoral College, Washington is indelibly marked as one of America's first patriots, as well as a true leader of the people.

George Washington's Birthplace. George Washington was born on a Virginia farm located on the shore of Bridges Creek in Westmoreland County on February 22, 1732. Later known as Wakefield, the house in which he was born burned down in 1799, but it is believed to have looked like the one seen here. Washington's father, Augustine, was a well-to-do tobacco farmer who owned three farms and about fifty black slaves. Mary Ball Washington had six children, including George, and also took care of Augustine's four children from his first marriage. The Washington family lived at Wakefield until about 1735.

Young George at School, ca. 1738. Though his older half-brothers were educated in England, young George was taught his lessons by the sexton of a local parish church, resulting in a somewhat rudimentary education. He would have trouble with his spelling all his life, but early on showed an aptitude for math. Like other children during that time, he practiced his handwriting by copying the 110 *Rules of Civility.* His other subjects included geography, astronomy, and arithmetic. By the time Washington reached his early teenage years, his formal education came to an end. However, he continued to learn the fundamentals of farming on his father's plantation, where his love of agriculture first began.

Chopping Down the Cherry Tree. Here we see an illustration of the often-told story in which George's father asks his son if he had killed a favored cherry tree. The young George confesses to his father, "I can't tell a lie, Pa; you know I can't tell a lie. I did cut it with my hatchet." Surprised and grateful, his father praised him for his honesty. In truth, there is no basis in fact for this legend. It was invented by Mason Locke Weems, a preacher who wrote the well-known *Life of George Washington* in the year 1800.

The Young Fox Hunter. As a young man, George Washington grew into a tall, strong athlete who excelled at sports and outdoor activities. He especially loved to hunt foxes with his hounds, as we see here. Originating in England, where foxes were considered a nuisance by sheep farmers, the sport of foxhunting was carried over to the colonies. In addition to hunting, Washington was also a superb horseback rider, prompting Thomas Jefferson to write that he was "the best horseman of his age."

An Apprentice Surveyor. At the age of 16, George Washington accompanied a surveying party to the Shenandoah Valley as an assistant, measuring the vast properties of Lord Fairfax, a wealthy and powerful Virginia landowner. By 17, he demonstrated enough skill and had gained the necessary knowledge to start his own business, and soon became commissioned as the official surveyor of Culpeper County. Here we see young Washington taking an azimuth sight as other assistants stake out boundary lines on the property being surveyed.

The Planter Aristocracy. The Virginia into which George Washington was born was a land of sprawling tobacco plantations owned by a class of rich planter aristocrats. Sent to England for their education, the planters observed the lavish lifestyles of their European brethren and brought this interest in fashion and entertainment back to the colonies.

Here we see a gala ball being held at a planter's grand plantation house. Unfortunately, this opulent way of life was largely supported by the profitable work of thousands of slaves in the tobacco fields. As an adult, Washington owned a number of slaves to work on his estate, but left instructions in his will to free them after his death.

Mount Vernon. In 1743, when George was 11, his father died. Washington became very close to his older half-brother, Lawrence, who lived on a farm on the Potomac River in Fairfax County. Lawrence named the new home "Mount Vernon" in honor of Edward Vernon, a British admiral under whom he had once served. Washington inherited the estate in 1752 upon Lawrence's death, and enlarged the original house, adding two wings and a third story. Here we see Mount Vernon as it looked in 1799.

A Young Volunteer Soldier. Since the late 17th century, France and England had been fighting a series of wars, collectively known as the French and Indian Wars, over the borders of their respective colonies, especially in North America. The colonists viewed this rivalry with apprehension, since their lands were often the sites of bloody raids and attacks. At age 21, George Washington was commissioned by Robert Dinwiddie, Royal Governor of the Virginia colony at Williamsburg, to deliver a letter to the commanding officer of the French forces occupying a section of the Ohio River. The ownership of the upper Ohio territory was disputed by the two antagonists, and Washington, as an agent of England, was sent to protest the building of two French forts in the region, and to possibly discover the intentions of the French army.

Crossing the Allegheny River. On the trip back to Williamsburg in February 1754, George Washington and his guide, Christopher Gist, had to journey hundreds of miles through the wilderness in raw winter weather. Their adventures included encounters with hostile Native Americans and a dangerous attempt to cross the Allegheny River by raft, as we see here. While fighting to navigate the crude raft around the ice floes, Washington was thrown into the frigid water and narrowly escaped drowning. The point of his crossing is now marked by a bridge, aptly named Washington's Crossing.

Marching Against the French. In 1754, French troops overtook and completed a partially-built British fortress in the wilderness of western Pennsylvania, naming it Fort Duquesne. The Governor of Virginia commissioned Lieutenant Colonel George Washington to lead a troop of 150 colonial soldiers to make a show of force and investigate French activities in the area, considered by many to be a part of the English colony. Washington joined forces with the Half-King, a Seneca chief who warned him on several occasions of the presence of French reconnaissance parties in the region.

A Morning Skirmish. In late May of 1754, guided by reports from the Half-King, George Washington led his troops in a morning ambush on a detachment of about thirty French soldiers. Badly outnumbered and with mounting casualties, the French attempted, but failed, to convey an intent to surrender to the young lieutenant colonel. His Native American allies were accused of scalping and murdering a number of the prisoners, and the affair was the event that touched off the French and Indian (or Seven Years) War in North America.

The Surrender of Fort Necessity. In anticipation of retaliation for the surprise attack, George Washington commanded his troops to hastily build a small stockade known as Fort Necessity. As expected, French troops amassed at Fort Duquesne in July 1754 and descended on the Virginian soldiers. Washington's troops—undisciplined, ill-equipped, and unpaid—struggled against the superior French arms with much difficulty. Outnumbered and hampered by bad weather, Colonel Washington eventually accepted the French emissary's terms of surrender, as we see here. Strong reactions to this defeat led to further hostilities between France and England over their North American colonies.

Braddock's Defeat. George Washington's next military action came when he joined British general Edward Braddock's campaign to oust the French from Fort Duquesne once and for all. Since he was familiar with the terrain and the enemy's fighting strategies, Washington attended General Braddock as a volunteer advisor.

Marching into the wilderness in July 1755, Braddock's army, comprised of 3,000 regular British troops and colonial soldiers, was ambushed by a French and Indian force on the banks of the Monongahela River, almost within sight of Fort Duquesne. Unused to the cunning tactics of the French and Indians, and disregarding the advice from

his young protégé, Braddock insisted on maintaining lines of soldiers on the open road, making them easy targets for the hidden opponents. Braddock was fatally wounded in this disastrous trap, leaving Washington, though ill with fever, to lead the retreat of the few surviving soldiers—less than two hundred—to safety. The next month saw Washington appointed by the Governor to be Commander-in-Chief of all the military forces of the colony of Virginia. In 1758, Washington commanded the advance guard of a British army that finally captured Fort Duquesne. At the end of the campaign, George Washington resigned his military commission and went home to Mount Vernon

George Washington Proposes. George Washington met Martha Dandridge Custis in 1758 while still a soldier. She had been married to Daniel Parke Custis, one of the wealthiest men in Virginia, but was widowed by the age of 26. She accepted Washington's proposal and brought a large dowry of $100,000 in gold, 7,500 acres of land, and over 300 slaves to their marriage.

Marriage of George Washington and Martha Custis. The couple's wedding took place at the bride's home on January 6, 1759, and was a grand social affair for the Virginia colonial aristocracy. With this marriage, Washington took over the management of Martha's substantial estate and became stepfather to her two young children by her first marriage. Washington was very fond of Patsy and Jack Custis, and treated them as his own children. With the combined estates, George Washington became, at age 27, one of the richest landowners in Virginia.

King George III. While George Washington was living the life of a gentleman farmer in rural Virginia, the thirteen North American colonies were undergoing a period of unrest. Though Britain had been victorious in the French and Indian War in 1763, its treasury was severely depleted from the years spent warring. King George III, seen here as he looked in 1775, decided to replenish his emptied coffers by taxing the colonists on items such as sugar, documents, paper, and tea. With no voice in the drafting of these policies, the colonists quickly became resentful of the new tariffs. They met in Congress and decided they must unite in their resistance to the king and his tyranny. However, George III was a monarch strongly determined to assert the rights of the Crown, and believed his protesting subjects in far-off America were fast approaching a dangerous condition of rebellion.

Washington Appointed Commander-in-Chief of Continental Army. As the political situation deteriorated, fighting between British troops and armed patriots called "Minute Men" broke out at the villages of Lexington and Concord in Massachusetts. Thousands of militiamen, composed mostly of angry farmers, began to assemble around Boston, besieging the British troops in the town. Members of the Second Continental Congress realized that, if rebellion was inevitable, a commander must be appointed to organize the armed mob into a structured army. They looked to George Washington—a former soldier experienced in warfare, and a man who could rally the southern colonies to unite with the northern and middle colonies in their common effort. On July 3, 1775, Washington was chosen by Congress to command the Patriot forces that had formed in New England. He accepted the post of Commander of the colonial forces but refused a salary, asking only that he be reimbursed for his expenses while fulfilling his commission.

Commanding the Patriot Forces. The force that Washington had been given to command was not an army, but a troop composed mainly of New England militia companies, Minute Men, farmers, backwoodsmen, shop keepers, drovers, and indentured servants (most of them runaways). A few veterans of the French and Indian War were present, but even they possessed little understanding of military strategy. Though the Patriots had the bravery and determination of the best of soldiers, they lacked the critical training and discipline of the British troops. As commander of the Patriot forces, George Washington was fated to be always the amateur warrior facing professional European soldiers.

Manufacturing the Weapons of War. Arming and outfitting the soldiers was the joint responsibility of the colonies and the Continental Congress. Both the colonies and Congress bought arms from local gunsmiths and purchased others from abroad. They also issued captured weapons and arms confiscated from Loyalists, who opposed the break from British rule. Here we see some Yankee gunsmiths making muskets for the local Committee of Safety, which issued contracts for the manufacture of weapons and military equipment for the Patriot forces.

Recruiting. During the first year of the war, enlistments for the new army were for a duration of six months or until the end of the conflict. Short enlistments such as this were in the militia tradition of the colonies from earlier wars, and most people thought that the problems with England would be resolved within a few months. In November 1775, with no end in sight, it was decided that further enlistments were to be extended for one year. By late 1776, men enlisted for three years or the duration of the war. It had become clear to all that the conflict would not be resolved in the immediate future. Here we see a recruiting station set up on the village green of a country town in 1775.

The Soldiers of a New Army. Training a new army was a formidable task. The men and boys that gathered to fight the English oppressors did not look or act like soldiers. They had few weapons and little gunpowder, and came and went as they chose, with little done to restrain them. Regional brawls erupted frequently between men from different colonies, with the inexperienced officers unable to establish order in the camps. To make matters worse, the men of this army served for only short periods of time and were free to go as soon as their military obligation was satisfied, resulting in more time spent recruiting and retraining new soldiers. With few supplies, no funds, and shortages of just about everything, George Washington had a difficult task before him. He did not even have the complete support of the Continental Congress, who made political appointments and granted promotions to officers without consulting him.

The War Begins. Various acts and laws passed by Parliament in London between 1770 and 1775 inflamed colonial unrest into open rebellion. By this time, the colonists came to realize that they were no longer English, but American, and armed conflict became inevitable. On June 17, 1775, British troops assaulted positions taken up by Patriot forces on Breed's Hill, outside Boston. A bloody clash ensued, commonly known as "The Battle of Bunker Hill" after a nearby site. Though technically a British victory, the ill-equipped colonists made an impressive effort by inflicting major casualties and fighting off the attacks. Most importantly, the Patriots discovered that they possessed the ability to resist the powerful British Army and possibly even defeat them. The American Revolution had begun. Here we see street boys abusing British troops as the marched through the streets of Boston in the spring.

Washington Reclaims Boston. In the weeks following the Battle of Bunker Hill, Washington arrived in Cambridge, near Boston, to take command of the Patriot forces in New England. By March, after months of training his army and acquiring weapons, Washington was ready to regain Boston from British control. Under his leadership, the Americans built up an enormous front of artillery on a hill overlooking Boston Harbor to threaten the British ships anchored there. Daunted by the great display of arms, the British quickly abandoned Boston and sailed to Nova Scotia to assess their situation. As the rebellion gained momentum, the British-appointed colonial governors either fled abroad or were imprisoned by the Patriot authorities. The old colonial system was collapsing and a new autonomous system was coming into being. Washington turned his attention to fortifying the port city of New York, essential to the critical control of the Hudson River and the northern and middle colonies.

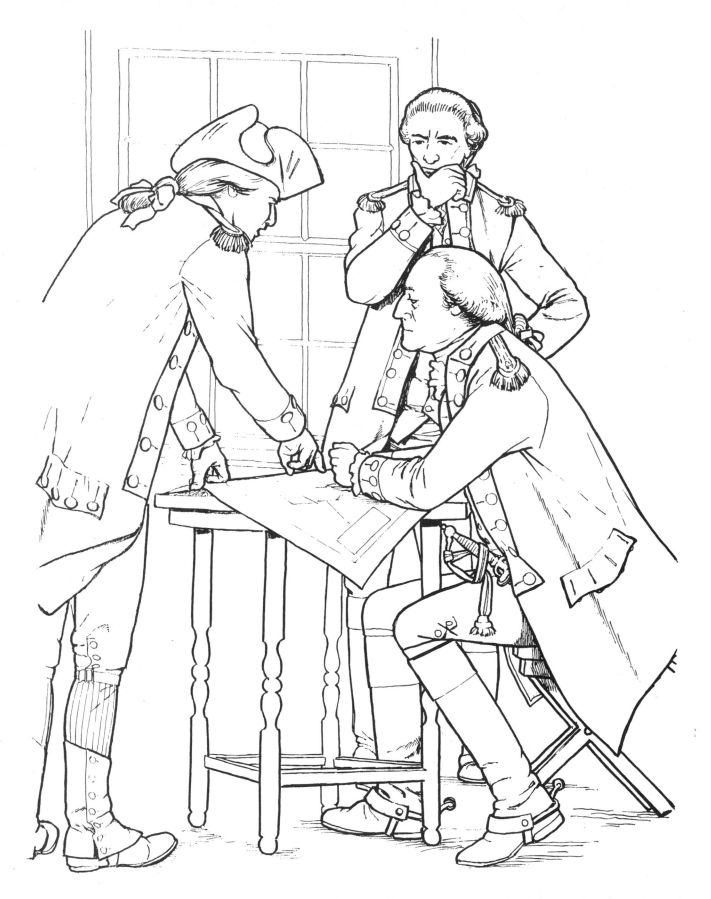

Planning Strategy. Congress proclaimed the signing of the Declaration of Independence on July 4, 1776. At that time, British convoys set off for America, carrying an army of thirty thousand British and Hessian troops and twelve hundred cannon, and escorted by a fleet of thirty Men of War. The impressive battalion was commanded by Sir William Howe, a general with an excellent army but little political strength. Washington, a general with an unreliable army, was now armed with a formidable political weapon—the Declaration of Independence. Here we see Washington reviewing tactical options with some of his officers.

Defeat at Long Island. In August 1776, the movement of the Patriot army from Boston to New York was hastily done. The British Army, in cooperation with the Royal Navy, moved to trap and destroy the Patriot lines. In a series of heavy battles, the British drove Washington's army out of New York and into the northern region. In November, British troops surrounded and captured Fort Washington, forcing the Patriots to retreat with a loss of approximately 4,000 men and crucial artillery. The casualties were high, but the moral defeat was even more devastating to the American cause. Had the British taken advantage of their victories, the revolution might have ended at this time.

Victory at Trenton. In the bitter cold of December 1776, George Washington's battered army launched a surprise attack on the Hessian garrison at Trenton, New Jersey. His troops crossed the ice-choked Delaware River and ambushed the encampment on December 26th, when the soldiers were still recovering from their Christmas festivities. Washington's force took the town and captured nearly a thousand Hessian soldiers, less than an hour after they first attacked. At last, the Continental Army had won a victory. Here we see Washington as he appeared in the famous but fanciful painting by Emanuel Leutze, done many years after the event it portrays. It is unlikely that Washington, a prudent commander, would have stood up in the bows of a boat being maneuvered across in ice-filled river. This is, however, certainly one of the most well-known depictions of Washington—accurate or not.

Washington at Princeton. Returning to Trenton in January 1777, the British endeavored again to trap Washington's army, surrounding the Continentals in an effort to push them against the Delaware River and defeat them. Washington led his troops on a midnight escape to Princeton, where he encountered another British detachment and attacked. When the outcome looked grim for the Patriots, Washington rode to the battlefront and rallied his wavering forces. The tide soon turned and the British were soundly routed for another major Continental victory. The Executive Council of Pennsylvania commissioned Charles Wilson Peale to paint a portrait of Washington to commemorate his victory, from which this drawing is copied.

Washington Greets Lafayette. The Marquis de Lafayette arrived in America in July 1777 and volunteered himself to Congress, offering to serve in the Continental Army without pay. Lafayette joined Washington's staff of officers, and the commander soon realized that this young French nobleman would be most valuable in helping to bring French assistance to the Patriot cause.

Von Steuben at Valley Forge. The hungry, ragged soldiers of the Continental Army marched into winter quarters at Valley Forge, Pennsylvania in December of 1777. In order to survive the bitter winter, the weary troops built cabins as shelter from the cold and snow. Despite their suffering, the American troops underwent a rigorous training program under Fredrich Von Steuben, a former Prussian officer. By spring, his discipline and instruction left the army a more professional and efficient force than it had ever been. Here we see the drill master Von Steuben giving instructions, via an interpreter, to a hapless recruit.

George Washington and the Continental Army.
Recruiting for the Continental Army remained a problem for Washington throughout the war. Most campaigns were fought using the Continental Army alongside local militia regiments, with mixed results. Several states instituted conscription, or the draft, in an effort to fill the thinning ranks, but without much success. Washington described his soldiers as ". . . half starved, always in rags, without pay, and experiencing every species of distress which human nature is capable of undergoing . . ." Here we see Generals Washington and Lafayette at Valley Forge.

Victory at Yorktown. After six long years of warfare and many defeats, fortune began to smile upon Washington and his army with the entrance of France into the war. The arrival of the French army and fleet enabled more strategic assaults on the British, and was a great help to the American forces. Outnumbered by the Franco-American army, the British were forced to surrender its troops at Yorktown in Virginia after losing the last major battle of the American Revolution. Here we see George Washington on October 9, 1781, firing the first gun from the allied artillery that opened the bombardment upon the British positions at Yorktown. On September 3, 1783, following British withdrawals and preliminary negotiations, the Treaty of Paris officially ended the Revolutionary War and America became an independent nation.

Farewell to the Army. On December 4, 1783, at a dinner at Fraunces Tavern in New York, Washington took formal leave of his officers. He then traveled to Annapolis, Maryland, where he resigned his commission on December 23. He stated, "Having now finished the work assigned me, I retire from the great theatre of Action; and bidding an Affectionate farewell to this August body under whose orders I have so long acted, I here offer my Commission, and take my leave of all the employments of public life." Washington then departed for Virginia to rejoin his beloved family and estate at Mount Vernon.

Coming Home. George Washington returned to Mount Vernon, eager to devote his time and energy to agriculture and the rebuilding of his dwindling estates, which had been neglected during eight years of war. During this quiet period, he conducted agricultural experiments, enlarged his home, and laid out new fields for planting. He did not, however, ignore public affairs in the new nation, and worried about the future of the United States without a plan of central government. Here we see Washington and his overseer supervising the work of field hands on the Mount Vernon estate.

A Family Man. Though himself childless, Washington enjoyed a full and warm family life. The two children of Martha Custis Washington's first marriage lived at Mount Vernon and were very dear to Washington. Upon the death of his stepson Jack, Washington adopted Jack's two children, Eleanor Park Custis ("Nelly"), and George Washington Custis. The children were devoted to Washington, and Nelly eventually married Washington's favorite nephew, Lawrence Lewis. Here we see Washington taking Nelly and George on a picnic, accompanied by a servant and his favorite Basset Hound, Putnam.

The Constitutional Convention. Now independent, the new nation was in need of a structured government. It was agreed that the existing Articles of Confederation needed to be replaced by a document that defined a strong federal body. In 1787, fifty-five delegates met to draft a new document, the Constitution of the United States of America, with George Washington quickly elected president of the convention. His belief was that, though imperfect, the Constitution must be adopted by the nation in order to preserve the union of states. Within two years, the Bill of Rights was added as a guarantee of individual liberty, perhaps the foremost principle for which the revolution was fought.

A Unanimous Choice. In February 1789, electors unanimously voted George Washington the first president of the United States. He was the one man who commanded the respect of all the regional factions—north and south, east and west—as well as the two contending political parties.

Washington, a southerner, was to be president, and John Adams, who hailed from the north, became his vice-president. Here we see Washington taking the oath of office in New York, the then-capital of the nation, administered by Chancellor Robert Livingston.

Washington as President, 1789-1793. The administration of George Washington was marked by caution, precision, and sober judgement—typical of the qualities he had always shown. He had a talent for picking the most suitable men to fill government positions, carefully balancing his appointments between the two newly formed political parties, liberal and conservative, refusing to align himself with either. Washington also respected the power of Congress and avoided encroaching on its authority, lest he become more dictator than president. He provided the newborn nation with the stability and leadership it needed during those formative years. Here we see the President and First Lady greeting guests at a State Reception.

The First Presidential Cabinet. Here we see Washington and members of his first cabinet (left to right): Washington; Henry Knox, Secretary of War; Alexander Hamilton, Secretary of the Treasury; Thomas Jefferson, Secretary of State; and Edmund Randolph, Attorney General. This group was chosen to evenly reflect the new

political divisions in the nation—those who believed in strong central government and others who supported states' rights. Washington was unhappy about the early divisiveness in the newly formed government, but, as a competent leader, accepted and incorporated the opposing parties in his administration.

The Second Term, 1793-1797. Washington had shown such genius for making men work together in his administration that he was re-elected for a second term as president. The turmoil of the French Revolution strongly influenced the American political scene, and as the two parties—Democrats and Federalists—became more clearly defined, political passions grew bitter. The Jay Treaty, regulating commerce and navigation, was causing new problems with

Great Britain, and Washington consequently came under increasing attack in the last years of his administration. At the close of his second term, Washington, weary of the political arena, chose not to seek a third term of presidency. In his farewell address on September 19, 1796, Washington urged citizens to avoid bipartisanship and remain neutral in foreign policy. Here we see Washington in a discussion with his advisors.

The Last Days. In 1797, Washington attended the inaugu-ration of John Adams as the second president of the United States. He then returned to Mount Vernon, thus ending his days of public service. However, he would not have many years to enjoy the peace of his beloved home. On December 14, 1799, stricken with pleurisy, Washington told his family, "I cannot last long," and died a few minutes later.

The Funeral. Washington's funeral service was a simple and small affair, attended only by friends, family, and neighbors at Mount Vernon. The father of his country had departed, leaving behind him an imperishable record of service and devotion. The nation grieved his passing from the date of his death to February 22, 1800, the official day of mourning. In that time, hundreds of commemorative speeches were given, including one by Washington's close associate, Henry Lee, who declared him to be "first in war, first in peace, and first in the hearts of his countrymen." Here we see the mile-long funeral procession on High Street in Philadelphia—one of many mock funerals held throughout the country. In a show of the nation's profound grief, a company of Philadelphia artificers conducted a riderless horse attired in mourning.

The Grave. Here we see the Washington family vault at Mount Vernon as it appeared in a mid-nineteenth century print. In his will, Washington directed his survivors to build the tomb according to his specific instructions. Over the doorway is the inscription, "Within this Enclosure Rest the remains of Gen. George Washington". In 1802, Martha took her place beside him in death.